The
Meditative Gardener
NOTEBOOK

themeditativegardener.blogspot.com

the
BLOGISATTVA
awards

WINNER

CHERYL WILFONG

Cheryl Wilfong
Heart Path Press, L3C
P.O. Box 336
Putney VT 05346
www.meditativegardener.com

©2010 Cheryl Wilfong

ISBN: 978-0-9825664-0-4

PHOTO ON COVER AND PAGE 1 BY LYNNE WEINSTEIN
PHOTO ON THIS PAGE BY GENE PARULIS
DESIGN BY DCDESIGN, BRATTLEBORO, VERMONT

*I*t takes time to discover the perfect meditation microclimate that fosters the flowering of your love for the Dharma.

*M*editation doesn't thrive in a busy, weedy mind, or in a bored, dry mind. Meditation succeeds when the mind is happy.

*S*itting regularly with a community of meditating friends is like companion planting—we support each other in our practice.

I propose that we first have goodwill toward our garden. Goodwill toward the very garden that grows outside our home right now. That garden is our refuge, our sanctuary where we meditate and contemplate and work and play.

The gardener of your garden is doing the best she can, using her time and knowledge to the best of her abilities. She may not get all the weeding done or all the seeds planted or all the plants watered, but she is doing the best she can, under the circumstances. She labors in your garden for the sheer love of it.

The seed of enlightenment is already growing in your heart. Meditation practice is the sunshine that warms the soil around that seed. A weekly sitting group nourishes that seed by watering the roots. Meditation books, such as the one you are holding in your hands, fertilize that seed of enlightenment sprouting in your heart of hearts.

*I*magine strolling through a garden and choosing the most beautiful flower. Feel its presence in your heart. Invite this blossom to grow in your heart.

Sitting comfortably in your yard or in a park and keeping your eyes partly open, allow your gaze to rest on a nearby plant, tree, or weed.

Say your loving-kindness phrases to this plant. "May you be safe. May you feel happy. May you feel strong. May you feel peaceful."

*I*s there a time of day when you stroll through your garden? Perhaps in the morning before work? Or after dinner, just before dusk? Choose a time when you walk for the sheer pleasure of enjoying your garden.

Go out and stand in one of your flower beds. Yes. Just stand there, inside the flower bed. Look around. How do you feel here? Pleasant? Unpleasant? Or neutral?

*I*t's easier to meditate if you are in pleasant surroundings. The heart is relaxed and happy, and perhaps a half-smile comes to the lips. So the garden can be an excellent place to meditate.

*I*n our meditation practice, we meditator-gardeners face the challenge of uprooting unwholesome thoughts and actions that cause stress or suffering. The Buddha identified three roots of stress: greed, aversion, and delusion.

*B*eing averse to aversion just waters the seeds of aversion and creates more of it, not less—sort of like scratching poison ivy.

*J*ust as mulch retains moisture and keeps the soil cooler in hot weather and warmer in cold weather, mindfulness can keep us cooler in hot-tempered situations and just a little warmer in cold, depressing times.

Simply recognizing a mental weed exposes its roots and shoots to the strong sunlight of mindfulness. Sometimes no further action is required, as you watch an unskillful thought simply wither.

The three roots of stress are counterbalanced by three wholesome roots. Specifically, the antidote to greed is generosity. The antidotes to aversion are loving-kindness and compassion. The antidote to delusion is wisdom itself.

*E*very time you give away a plant, a cutting, or some seeds, you are practicing generosity.

Learning to receive with an open heart is as important as learning to give in an open-handed manner.

Receiving a gift graciously allows the giver to experience the joy of giving. Joy is such a wholesome emotion, it is so beneficial, that it is one of the seven factors for awakening. Joy can wake us up.

You multiply your plants by dividing them.

Gardening is an experiential practice.
So is meditation.

When we understand that the noun "garden" is a concept, that "garden" is actually a slow-moving verb of ever-changing flowers, plants, conditions, and even soil, then we can glimpse the emptiness of the garden.

$\mathcal{T}$homas Jefferson wrote, "Though an old man, I am but a young gardener." This beginner's mind is a great attitude to cultivate for your meditation practice.

$\mathcal{A}$t the end of your next sitting meditation, drop
this wish into the pond of your still reflection:
"May I see things as they truly are."

*G*ardeners know about being patient, whether or not they are good at it. Despite our desires for quick results, that new perennial just planted will not be hurried into lushness. In fact, the perennials we cultivate usually follow this adage:

The first year they sleep,

The second year they creep.

The third year they leap.

Our meditation practice cannot be rushed
along. Unfortunately it does not come with a
note that tells us exactly how long it will be
before we can expect to reap the fruits of our
practice, but patience does guarantee that if the
seed of mindfulness is watered and cultivated,
our practice bears fruit.

Doing something which benefits your garden
(or yourself), even though you may not want to,
requires determination.

*T*ruth is a commitment to what is real—
it is rooted in the soil of reality rather than
illusion. Wisdom is the realization of truth.
We immediately know when an insight is true,
because our body understands it as well as
our mind.

Let's begin with the practice of goodwill toward our garden and goodwill toward our gardener, our self.

$\mathcal{E}$quanimity is this acceptance of the things we cannot change—whether our health, our partner, the decisions of our family members, our out-of-control gardens, or the policies of our government. It's important to keep in mind that equanimity is acceptance, not indifference.

Generosity and renunciation condition the mind to let go of greedy attachments and desires.

*R*elaxing into patience and cultivating loving-kindness expand the narrow and aversive mind.

*W*isdom and equanimity shed light on
ignorance and the delusional mind.

*O*ur entire spiritual path sprouts from a root system of ethics. Nourishing the healthy roots of a virtuous life enables us to continue walking our walk without stumbling on the stones of regret or remorse.

Suffering is the impetus that drives many of us toward a spiritual path.

$\mathcal{T}$he precept of refraining from destroying living creatures encourages us to develop the wholesome habit of harmlessness, but as a gardener, you may have some serious questions to ponder in your own heart.

I really do enjoy liberating the creatures I find inside my home and sending them back to their native country where they can be free to live their own lives.

*I*magine your favorite insect and say your loving-kindness phrases to it. "May you feel safe. May you feel happy. May you feel strong. May you feel peaceful."

*I*f we want to practice ethical gardening, we need to look deeply into our gardening practices and ask ourselves whether what we are doing today will cost or benefit future generations.

The precept of using our sexual energy wisely encourages us to relate harmlessly to one another by being trustworthy and responsible.

A contemplating mind grazes within a
fenced-in meadow, unlike the discursive mind,
which gallops off over the prairie.

Giving the mind something to investigate, such as a contemplation, can enliven, deepen, and strengthen your meditation practice, particularly if the mind has lost interest in the body or feelings.

*I*gnoring the facts of life does not mean they will not happen. Ignoring them leads simply to ignor-ance.

We gardeners have our fingers on the pulse of life as we watch hundreds of flowers bloom, age, perhaps become sick, and die every gardening season. We know at a visceral level that we human beings also have a life cycle. We, too, are part of the cycle of life.

*T*hink of a relative—a parent, grandparent, or other family member—or a friend from whom you inherited your gardening "gene."

Recall the span of her gardening life, and (if you know) how it changed over the years.

When Ruth Stout was more than 90, the still-spirited, but now frail nonagenarian sat in front of the upscale garden club in her worn-out chenille bathrobe. Someone asked her, "Where do you store your winter squash?"

Without missing a beat, Ruth quipped, "Under the kitchen table."

*A*s gardeners we are face to face with death every day that we are in the garden, whether it's plants, insects, or just a dying blossom. We know that one of these days, we ourselves will be pushing up daisies.

I have heard of someone who collects the plant markers of departed plants, gathering them like little white plastic tombstones.

*E*very day I make at least one trip to the compost pile, which is the graveyard for my plants and vegetables.

Watering the seeds of anger creates more anger. Watering the seeds of greed creates more greed—the feeling of never having enough. Watering the seeds of delusion creates more ignorance.

What actually satisfies desire is not obtaining
the next new plant but stopping desire itself.
This may sound like a koan.
How can you stop desire without satisfying it?

$\mathcal{A}$ friend took her grandson to a retreat center with a prayer wheel. Now her grandchild delights in dandelion seed puffs, calling them flower prayer wheels.

Often weeds are communicating something to us about the soil. What's the message your weeds are sending you?

Sloth and torpor are like a stagnant pond; energy is stuck. The traditional remedy is to live in open air, change posture, and change light. It sounds as if gardening itself is the cure.

$\mathcal{W}$anting to know the unknowable future gives rise to anxiety, because that sense desire (of the mind) can never ever be satisfied.

You don't need much faith—just enough to take you out to the garden today or enough to sit to the end of your meditation. Just enough to follow through on your decision to garden with a meditative mind.

The factors for awakening form a habitat. When one grows, the others will also naturally arise, one after the other.

*T*he seven factors for awakening have the capacity to stop the show. The "show" is delusion itself.

$\mathcal{A}$s a gardener I appreciate cultivating an environment where wholesome seeds and wholesome roots can grow and bloom and where weeds slowly but surely diminish and can even be entirely uprooted.

What energizes your meditation—
or your gardening?

*O*ur gardens must bring us some form of happiness; otherwise we would not continue getting ourselves hot, dirty, sweaty, and bitten by bugs for the sake of a few flowers or vegetables.

$\mathcal{A}$s gardeners, we continue to exert energy on a regular basis, and that energy brings us the joy of being in the garden, the joy of seeing flowers bloom, cutting flowers for a bouquet, harvesting and eating our very own vegetables.

$\mathcal{W}$e need to en-joy some aspect of meditating; otherwise we will never sit down long enough to practice.

Remember to say a few words of thanks before dining on your garden feast. Over time gratitude for all things large and small feeds the feeling of joy.

*I*magine being as absorbed in meditation as you can be in the garden.

I go about my weeding and transplanting and dead-heading with the full knowledge that this garden I love is subject to all sorts of changes.

*A*s you go out to your garden today, say,
*"I dedicate this garden to the awakening of
all beings."*

The bumper sticker "Practice random kindness and senseless acts of beauty" speaks to the impartial nature of loving-kindness.

$\mathcal{A}$nd then there's the bumper sticker that says, "Practice random acts of gardening."

War is commemorated in some park in every town and city in America and on at least three of our national holidays, yet monuments to peace and peace gardens are few and far between.

While visiting someone else's garden, how often does the comparing mind leap to the fore? "My flower beds don't look that good," the mind says, or "My gardens are better than this," as if gardening was a contest and there could be only one winner.

*J*ust imagine "appreciating" your friend's garden—recognizing with gratitude the effort she puts into it and thereby increasing the personal value of her effort.

The quality of equanimity relies on a deep understanding of karma, which, in gardener's language, translates as, "You reap what you sow."

The divine abodes shower loving-kindness, compassion, appreciative joy, and equanimity on all beings, impartially.

$\mathcal{T}$he middle way is not a linear path. It's more like a hologram with many entrances.

*M*indfulness is the key to our secret garden.

Breinigsville, PA USA
25 April 2010
236736BV00002B/1/P